SOUL MATES
AND
TWIN FLAMES

Soul Mates
and
Twin Flames

*The Spiritual Dimension of
Love and Relationships*

Elizabeth Clare Prophet

Summit University Press®

SOUL MATES AND TWIN FLAMES
The Spiritual Dimension of Love and Relationships
by Elizabeth Clare Prophet.

Copyright © 1999 by Summit University Press.

ISBN 0-922729-48-4

SUMMIT UNIVERSITY ⚘ PRESS®
Summit University Press and ⚘ are registered trademarks.
Printed in the United States of America.

03 02 01 00 99   6 5 4 3 2 1

CONTENTS

CONTENTS

*I am my beloved's,
and my beloved is mine.*

SONG OF SOLOMON 6:3

*I will rise now, and go about the
city in the streets, and in the broad ways
I will seek him whom my soul loveth:
I sought him, but I found him not.
The watchmen that go about
the city found me: to whom I said,
Saw ye him whom my soul loveth?
It was but a little that I passed from
them, but I found him whom my
soul loveth: I held him, and
would not let him go.*

SONG OF SOLOMON 3:2–4

THE
PERFECT MATCH
TRAPPED IN THE NET OF KARMA

THE STORY OF
Jeanette MacDonald
Nelson Eddy

Sweetheart, sweetheart, sweetheart," Nelson Eddy sang. Suddenly from the rear of the theater came the voice of a woman, joining him in duet. The packed audience turned in amazement. She was walking down the aisle, singing back to him. By the end of the song, she was on stage looking into his eyes and the audience was standing and cheering.

I

She was his co-star in eight films, Jeanette MacDonald. Their love was plain for all to see, recalls Frank Laric, who was sitting in the third row. Nelson hadn't even known she was in town. "Where'd you come from?" he asked as the audience wildly applauded.

"I got in last night," she said. He asked her to dinner, and then they sang "Indian Love Call" together.

In these magic moments and in those replayed in theaters across the nation, America discovered twin flames.*

 $\mathcal{I}$ t was the summer of 1941. Theirs was the perfect match and more, twin flames to a T —two hearts in three-quarter time. Although their romance blossomed in May, it never came to fruition.

---

*Twin flames are souls who were created together in the beginning, two halves of a divine whole. See pages 39–50.

Seeing their love on screen, hearing it in their duets as their eyes told one another and the whole world the pain of a forbidden love, more than one generation of Americans have been introduced to that special love of twin flames. Although not many people today sit down and listen to Jeanette and Nelson sing arias, their music and especially their films have a timeless appeal, which transcends a bland corniness in plot and dialogue. That appeal, that mysterious ingredient, is the love that everyone seeks, but few find, in the union of twin flames.

Yet they were forced to hide that real-life romance from the world. Official studio history and fan magazines billed them as casual friends who sometimes argued and who were blissfully married to other people.

And that story might have stood forever had it not been for the efforts of Sharon Rich

Not a publicity photo. This shows their real-life romance as Nelson throws caution to the winds and gives Jeanette a birthday embrace.

and Diane Goodrich who released their book *Farewell to Dreams* in 1979. They compiled it not from the papier-mâché newspaper accounts of the day, but from Nelson's and Jeanette's friends, neighbors, and relatives who finally agreed to tell the truth and from doormen, maids, and extras who filled in details and corroborated evidence. "Every line in there," Sharon says, "is verbatim from what somebody told us, as closely as possible."

Sharon and Diane discovered a massive cover-up by the studio and by Nelson and Jeanette, who swore their friends to secrecy. They found that they were in fact wildly in love, more deeply than any of their characters, in a romance that spanned 30 years.

But Jeanette's ambition, their occasionally violent tempers, and a strange combination of people and circumstances kept them apart for their entire lives. So it seems that things do not always turn out right, even when you do find your twin flame.

Their life story is a tragedy of twin flames. It includes an implicit warning to us in our quest for our perfect love: if we do not overcome the negatives of our karma, we can never enjoy complete happiness, whether or not we find our twin flame.

$\mathcal{N}$aturally, Sharon and Diane's story begins as a fairy tale should: love at first sight, or at least instant recognition. Jeanette's sister Blossom was flipping through a newspaper when a picture caught her eye. "Who is that?" said Jeanette, making her go back to a certain page. She knew she had to go and hear Nelson Eddy sing.

Nelson first saw, or rather heard, Jeanette at MGM studios where they were both under contract. He had been signed on in 1933, a successful opera singer and—as young, handsome opera singers were in those days —a sex symbol. His fans, mostly women, treated him like a rock star, even ripping his clothes off after concerts.

Nelson followed her bewitching voice into a sound stage where she was filming *The Merry Widow*. As he watched her on stage, he fell in love. She fit the image of that one girl he'd always dreamed of. A few days later, he asked her to lunch. She agreed, but only reluctantly as she did not want to become entangled in a relationship that might endanger her career. Yet as their romance continued, her love grew. Nelson made her, a 30-year-old glamour queen, feel like she was on her first date. Could the fairy tale she had portrayed so many times on screen be happening to her?

"He kissed me, it's like nothing I ever felt before," she told her mother. "Around him

I feel beautifully elated, and when he looks at you, there's no one else, just you."

*I*n their romance we see other telltale signs of a twin flame relationship. Their love was far more than a magnetic attraction—it showed in every part of their lives. Together, they had a radiance that was lacking when they were apart. The films they made singly are mostly unmemorable, but together they were able to tap their inner potential as twin flames united can, and their films broke box-office records.

Their radiant screen presence, the very real quality of their love and the now-revealed pathos of their separation made the eight movies the MacDonald/Eddy team filmed from 1935 to 1942 some of the most poignant love stories ever portrayed by Hollywood.

Their popularity is timeless. MGM re-released several of their films in the late '50s and early '60s and recently put out three of them on video. Their loyal fans, young and old, still rally around their three fan clubs, one the oldest in existence.

Their love did not fade as their bodies grew older. He still saw her as she had looked on their first meeting. "Beauty comes from the soul," Nelson said in 1958. "The body is just a cover. Sure, it ages and gets worn. But it's the person himself who radiates beauty, or doesn't. That's why I'll care for Miss MacDonald till the day I die." Feeling his love, Jeanette would light up like a firefly whenever he was near, becoming a different person in his presence.

Their undying love, another sign of twin flames, extended beyond that one life, or so they believed.

Sharon and Diane discovered that both believed in reincarnation. In the 1930s, a psychic told Jeanette that she had known Nelson before when they lived as brother and sister in the 1830s in England. On the trail of the MacDonald/Eddy story, Diane Goodrich went to another psychic, saying nothing of what Jeanette had learned, and this psychic gave exactly the same reading.

Although it is easy to expect that twin flames would always be lovers, that is not necessarily the case. A brother-sister relationship does not preclude a soul mate or twin flame bond, as the love of twin flames stretches beyond one or two lifetimes back to the point of creation.

In the brother-sister mode, it can establish a bond of commitment and pristine love, a mutual adoration and achievement. It is a very real part of the spiral that builds, lifetime after lifetime, between twin flames preparing for that ultimate union wherein the fruit of their love becomes a unique contribution upon the altar of humanity. A love so powerful as to elevate and ennoble all it touches and to purify and renew the stream of mankind's awareness of what true love can be and conquer.

Jeanette and Nelson also believed in karma—that they were responsible for the current circumstances of their lives, which were the result of their past actions. They must have had a fair amount of karma between them, as twin flames often do, for, as it turns out, the course of their love did not run smoothly.

Their story has a villain—an ugly stepmother, a troll beneath the bridge. It came packaged in the form of megalomaniac Louis

B. Mayer, the power broker of MGM. When Nelson fell in love with Jeanette, the fledgling star was in the usual sexual submission to her patron, and he did not like the "baritone." For one thing, Nelson had already been successful in his own right and did not owe his career to MGM. Therefore, he was the only star on the lot who didn't kowtow to Louis.

Anna MacDonald, Jeanette's mother, and Louis were quick to point out to her that she risked all she had worked so hard for by falling for "a mere singer."

Frightened for her career, she began pretending to ignore Nelson. But he made it clear that he didn't care what her past contained, including a relationship to Louis. "What we have together cannot be lightly dismissed. . . . When the chips are down and you want someone who really cares, just remember I'm real," he said.

They began filming *Naughty Marietta*, their first film together, in 1935. When it became apparent it would be a hit, making Jeanette a superstar, Louis gave her her freedom. He didn't like to sleep with his stars—it might spoil their reputation. But he still had it in for her new boyfriend.

During the last half of the filming, Nelson and Jeanette's love grew and blossomed. "Around him she felt strangely pure and naïve," *Farewell to Dreams* tells us.

They both knew it was far more than just a fling. "From the very first time I saw her, that was it. She answered every unspoken thought, every desire I've ever dreamed. It's as if I cannot be, I cannot exist without her," Nelson later told "Pop" Leonard, their director.

When *Naughty Marietta* became one of

the top films of the year, the public clamored for more MacDonald/Eddy. By the time they began their second film, *Rose Marie,* which features "Indian Love Call" ("When I'm call-ing you ou ou ou ou ou ou"), they were madly in love, all pretense forgotten, and

Rose Marie, 1936

Jeanette had never been so happy in her life.

Like true soul partners, they brought out the best in each other—he assisting her in singing and she helping him with acting. To their director, cast, and crew it was clear: They had been made for each other.

*A*t Lake Tahoe, the film site, their love progressed down a primrose path. They rode horses together, made love, he asked her to marry him and she accepted. She adored the beautiful emerald ring encircled by diamonds he gave her. "Oh, Nelson, I promise I'll wear it forever. That way you'll always be near me." But, always the star, she wanted to wait until June and have a big wedding.

And this was to cost them all, for looming beneath the calm sea of their love was the rock of ambition on which their lives were to be wrecked. Sharon and Diane give us this scene:

Soon Jeanette discovered she was pregnant. He was ecstatic, wanting an immediate wedding, but she was irritated with him for not understanding. In those days if a female star got married or pregnant in or out of wedlock without the studio's permission, her contract was null and void.

As the reality of karmic circumstance surrounded her like a concrete wall, the pressure became too great. To have a baby, she thought, would destroy her. "I won't have you ruin my career! ... Get this through your head... I don't want your puling brat, and that's final!" she railed.

"You—you—you don't know what you're saying! That's not you talking, Jenny. I won't believe that all you want from life is to be a big star. It's such an empty thing."

"That's exactly what I do want, and I'll do anything—anything—to get there. Do you hear? Anything! I'm going to be the biggest star around and nobody's going to stop me! Do you understand?"

"By all means keep your career. Let's see how much love and warmth it'll give you."

That scene was the sounding of the death knell to any enduring happiness they might have enjoyed. The next day Jeanette had a miscarriage. She tried to patch things up, but Nelson was still angry and disillusioned. He rebuffed her and promptly attached himself to a little blonde starlet, Anita Louise.

Out to prove that two could play that game, Jeanette called up Gene Raymond, an actor whom she had dated a few times, and invited him to Lake Tahoe. He was so charming and supportive of her career that, when he took her by surprise with a marriage proposal, she found herself accepting. He would not thwart her ambitions. "Your career is all that matters," he told her. For reasons not entirely clear, she accepted his proposal, not anticipating the next act in the tragedy for which she alone had set the stage.

Gene immediately called MGM and announced the wedding. Louis was delighted, seeing in this a chance to get back at his insubordinate baritone. His star was getting married. He decided to plan the "biggest publicity caper ever."

During the filming of *Maytime,* their next film, the lovers made up and tried to call off the wedding but Louis refused, threatening to ruin Jeanette. In desperation, Nelson offered Gene $250,000 to break off the engagement. He happily accepted but Louis once again intervened, apparently threatening Gene's life. Louis, who reigned absolute over his stable of stars, was not given to idle threats. "I want to go on living for awhile yet," Gene said, backing out.

Nelson was in despair. With him relying on alcohol and Jeanette on tranquilizers, they

Maytime, 1937

somehow got through the ordeal of filming.

The plot of *Maytime* filled Nelson with a sense of foreboding. He believed they had ruined their lives before and were repeating the pattern now. His dread was that the story they were acting out would come true.

In the film, a rising opera star, Marcia Mornay, agrees to a loveless marriage with her music teacher, Nicolai. That night in Paris she meets a young singer, Paul Allison, whom she realizes is her true love, spends one beautiful May Day with him, but decides she will still marry Nicolai out of obligation. She stays with him for seven miserable years, then meets Paul again in New York.

Realizing she is still desperately in love, she asks Nicolai for her freedom. He agrees, but all too easily. Leaving her, he takes a gun, finds Paul and kills him. She arrives on the scene moments after only to hear him say,

"That day did last me all my life."

In the end, alone and elderly, her soul, in springtime reverie, takes leave of the body as he comes to her singing. She takes his out-stretched hand and their spirits, at last united, walk away into the blossoming May.

Nelson's fears were not unfounded. As Jeanette appeared determined to go ahead with the ceremony, his last hope was to kid-nap her. He came to her house just before the wedding and dragged her downstairs and into his car.

"Jenny, tell me you don't love me! Look me in the eye and tell me. If you can do that, I'll believe you and I'll never bother you again." Jeanette eyed him defiantly at first, but her gaze faltered. She turned away in an effort to hide her tears. Seeing them, Nelson drew her to him. She stiffened and shrank back, stammering. "No—no, I can't. I won't let you do this. It can't make up for my career. Don't you understand that? Love's important, but…"

Nelson's voice echoed his desperation. "Angel, Angel, what is there in you that only destroys us? People search all their lives for what we have, and you're willing to throw it all away with your wanton greediness."

Moved by his agony, she stepped closer to him, then caught herself and screamed, "No, no, it's all arranged! The biggest wedding ever! My fans—I can't, I can't—I love my career more!" He let her go, realizing he had lost her.

The wedding must have been one of the most crushing moments in Nelson's life. Guests remember his choked sobs filling the church throughout the ceremony. As planned, he sang "I Love You Truly" soon after the opening lines, "Dearly Beloved, we are gathered together here in the sight of God and in the face of this company to join together this man and this woman in holy matrimony..." —words he never thought he would hear with tears in his eyes.

His imploring rendition of the song mirrored her singing of "Indian Love Call" to him in Rose Marie when he, as a Canadian Mountie, arrests her brother. With the most impassioned plea in the history of film, she begs him if he loves her to turn back. Neither in the wedding nor on film did either swerve from their chosen course, but the movie at least had a happy ending.

No sooner had she gotten to Hawaii with her new husband, than she discovered her terrible mistake: he was gay. She threatened to have the marriage annulled; he threatened that if she went back to Nelson, he would plaster the scandal across every front page.

$\mathcal{J}$eanette was caught between two ages. In the harsher standards of the '30s where movie stars were paragons of perfection, she determined not to mar her angelic image and once again chose fame over personal happiness. Jeanette sadly resigned herself to the rocky road she had taken, realizing with increasing despair that she had ruined her life and Nelson's... She knew it was all her fault, that Nelson really was real, the sweetest guy she'd ever known, and the only one who had ever loved her truly. The guilt would gnaw at her to the end of her days.

Meanwhile, Louis' publicity machine was grinding out stories of the Raymonds' marital bliss and the fan magazines and gossip columns were full of it. They kept up the façade, attending social functions arm-in-arm and playing the role of the happy couple.

Nelson and Jeanette filmed *Girl of the Golden West,* woodenly doing their jobs. It is their only film without a love duet, as she couldn't sing "Obey Your Heart," written for the movie, without breaking down. By the next film, *Sweethearts,* the situation for her was becoming intolerable.

According to Diane and Sharon, one night she went out looking for Gene to keep a social engagement and finally found him in bed in a gay club. Jeanette collected his clothes and dragged him out to the sneers of other gay couples.

That night she went back to Nelson "for good," moving out of her house a few days later when Gene hit her, badly bruising her face. Nelson, always fiercely protective of her, beat up Gene soundly enough to send him to the hospital for two weeks. The love-birds moved into a cottage in Burbank and played at being normal people. Neighbors still remember them as "that nice married couple who liked to ride horses."

Jeanette filed for divorce and *Sweethearts* continued, both of them now demonstrating their love in every word and glance. She became blissfully pregnant and this time they

Sweethearts, 1938

both wanted an instant marriage. They planned a home together in Bel Air with a nursery done in pink and lavender; all their dreams were about to come true.

Until Louis saw them together and realized they were in love. Furious was not the word. Jeanette told him that Gene was a homosexual, that she'd had enough, and that she was getting a divorce; Louis forbade it.

"*I* understand, but the box office won't understand. . . . Tell me another word and I'll destroy you both." But both Jeanette and Nelson stood firm.

Nevertheless, Louis' threats had the desired effect. The next day Jeanette collapsed and fell down the high ramp on which the musical extravaganza was being filmed. She was six months pregnant. Nelson picked her up and took her to the hospital, her dress soaked in blood. She had a miscarriage, he collapsed, and they awoke to the news that she could never have another child. The baby, a boy, lived for two days.

Louis' threats again kept them apart. He told Jeanette that if they didn't stop seeing each other, Nelson would be found "floating on his face feeding the fishes. . . . Either you straighten up or I'll sic my boys on him, and I'm not fooling." As Louis had not-too-well hidden ties to the underworld, she believed him.

Jeanette returned to Gene without telling Nelson of her decision. Characteristically, he internalized the pain, declaring he never wanted to see her again. He went into a tailspin, keeping irregular hours, drinking, and finally getting sick.

Then, *Farewell to Dreams* reports, the story took another strange twist. Ann Franklin, a casual acquaintance, dropped by Nelson's house with a deliberate plot in mind. She got him drinking, which, combined with his depression and medication-induced fuzziness, weakened his will. She asked him to marry her. He, always an irrational drunk, agreed. After all, Jeanette wasn't the only one who could get married. He awoke on the train going home from Las Vegas to the voice of his new bride. He had no recollection of the event and ever thereafter averred that the judge must have been bribed to have married a man in that state.

Sharon Rich discovered that Ann, in order to prevent Nelson from later annulling the marriage, had had incriminating pictures taken to prove that it had been consummated.

When Jeanette heard the news, she tried to kill herself, taking almost an entire bottle of sleeping pills. She gradually recovered and soon began production of *New Moon* (1940).

They were cool to each other at first, then rediscovered their love and decided they couldn't be apart.

She moved back to their little house but Louis found out again. He forced them apart: "The only time I want to see you two together is in front of the camera, no place else." During that film, they were forced to go through the agony of staying on opposite sides of the set. But he couldn't keep them apart for long. They began seeing each other again, vowing to be more careful.

Finally things came to a head when Ann Eddy went to Louis and complained about her ever-absent husband. Louis got furious and called Jeanette a whore. Nelson nearly strangled him and quit, buying out his studio contract. Jeanette did convince him to finish out their current and last film, *I Married an Angel* (1942).

*J*eanette's career now meant little or nothing to her beside her love for Nelson. She ceased to be as exacting of herself and consequently her performance suffered. Louis decided not to pick up the option on her contract.

Although she made three more films and gave a number of plays, war benefits, concerts and actually sang opera as she had always dreamed, her career never picked up to full steam.

Their public lives were now reversed. Jeanette was too old to play a romantic lead but Nelson was still in demand. He made four more well received films and continued giving concerts and doing nightclub acts for the rest of his life.

In 1946, Jeanette suffered a nervous breakdown. From there on, her health was a constant problem. In 1948 she had her first heart attack.

During this latter period, both Nelson and Jeanette were apathetic about fixing up their lives. It was as though things had already gone too far and they might as well wait for the next round and another opportunity.

He had to keep working because his wife had either tied up or spent all his money. He didn't even have enough to buy Jeanette and himself a house in Scottsdale, Arizona, where they planned to retire together.

In the meantime, the twin flames of stardom lived on with their respective spouses. Which brings up one of the unanswered questions of their story: why didn't they each get a divorce? By 1950, surely divorce was not such a stigma as it had been in 1937.

On Nelson's side, Ann refused to give him his freedom although he begged her. Jeanette probably stayed with Gene out of sympathy in response to his carefully contrived "I'll-never-do-it-again" weeping scenes, begging for forgiveness on bended knee.

Another reason Jeanette and Nelson may not have divorced their 'paper mates' is that they were already married! Since publishing her book, Sharon Rich has uncovered evidence which leads her to believe that Nelson was already married to Jeanette when he married Ann! Some of her sources mentioned that Jeanette and Nelson had gone down to Mexico to get married. Sharon believes this took place while Jeanette was pregnant during the filming of *Sweethearts*. This is especially plausible because the strong-minded Nelson, if true to character, would never have allowed his baby to be born with another man's name.

In Mexico, they could have gotten a proxy divorce without Gene present and been married quickly. Then, when Nelson married Ann, she may have blackmailed him with the charge of bigamy. That would have been enough to keep him tied to her for life. Now divorce would have created a scandal with reverberations casting a shadow not only on Jeanette's career, but also on her morality.

Thus, the fact that now neither one tried to hide their continuing love for each other may be explained by their sense of its rightness as well as its lawfulness secured by marriage, albeit secret.

Their devotion spanned the miles. Once, when Nelson received a slightly disturbing letter from Jeanette while on tour in Australia, he canceled his engagements and flew back to Hollywood because he had a bad feeling about it. When he discovered she was OK (or pretended to be), he felt sheepish.

At some point, Gene began to take more control of her life, forcing her to sell their house and move into an apartment. Nelson was constantly traveling, unaware of her deteriorating physical condition, for she kept from him till the end her painfully bad (broken) heart.

She wasted away slowly as Gene and the maid neglected to feed her and took away her phone to prevent her from calling Nelson. Gene gave her sleeping pills much of the time to keep her quiet. If she had not had the tremendous guilt gnawing at her, she might have had more interest in living, but, as her sister Blossom said, "It was the guilt that killed her."

*W*hen she died on January 14, 1965, Gene was at her bedside. Delirious, she thought he was Nelson. With her last breath she said across eternity to the one who had loved her soul from the beginning, "I love you."

Like Romeo, Nelson sought to follow his Juliet, but he was thwarted in his every

attempt at self-destruction. Finally, he collapsed during a show in Florida two years
after her death and died a few hours later. We
may hope that as in *Maytime* she greeted
him with a song as he stepped lightly out of
his careworn body.

In realms of light they could await their
next entrance on the stage of life, a chance
to build their lives anew, this time to make
the choice to conquer pride and ambition—
for Love. And in a place where the Louis B.
Mayers or Gene Raymonds or Ann Franklins
would have no power over their spirits: for
they had truly been tried and made white in
the fires of their self-induced adversity. Wise
to the forces that assail real Love and, above
all, protective of their marriage made in
heaven, they would realize on earth their most
sacred secret hope—to be one forevermore.

And nothing and no one would come

between them—for without Love, life is "as sounding brass or tinkling cymbal (I Cor. 13:1).... For now we see through a glass darkly but then face to face." (I Cor. 13:12) And the decree of the LORD God upon the twin flames he had made would not be denied: "What therefore God hath joined together let no man put asunder." (Matt. 19:6)

PICTURE CREDITS: Pictures courtesy of the collection of Sharon Rich.

For more information about the lives and romance of Jeanette and Nelson, contact the Mac/Eddy Club, P.O. Box 1077, New York, NY 10002, email to maceddy@earthlink.net or visit their website at http://home.earthlink.net/~maceddy/index.html. Excerpts from *Farewell to Dreams* by Diane Goodrich and Sharon Rich, copyright 1979, the Jeanette MacDonald/Nelson Eddy Friendship Club, Inc., are used with permission. That book is now out of print, but Sharon Rich has updated her research with even more documentation, including love letters, in a newer book, *Sweethearts: The Timeless Love Affair—On Stage and Off—Between Jeanette MacDonald and Nelson Eddy*, published by Donald I. Fine, 1994, available through the above website.

THE QUEST
FOR WHOLENESS

*E*ach one of us has a twin soul, or twin flame, who was created with us in the beginning. God created you and your twin flame out of a single "white fire body." He separated this white fire ovoid into two spheres of being—one with a masculine polarity and the other with a feminine polarity, but each with the same spiritual origin and unique pattern of identity.

Aeons ago, you and your twin flame stood before the Father-Mother God and volunteered to descend into the planes of matter to bring God's love to earth. The original plan was that you would go through a series of incarnations in both masculine and feminine embodiments, as each half of the Divine Whole learned to be the instrument of the Father-Mother God.

Our early life on earth was blissful, and we would each have continued to share the beauty of the relationship of cosmic lovers with our twin flame throughout our many incarnations, if we had remained in harmony with each other and with God. But we fell from the state of perfection by misusing God's light. This is the true meaning of the Garden of Eden story.

Had we retained the harmony of the One, the rapture of our love would have remained throughout our lifetimes on earth. But when harmony was lost—through fear, mistrust, or a sense of separation from our Source—we became the victims of our negative karma. Separated vibrationally, no longer preferring one another, we were bound by entangling alliances and mutual neglect until our souls cried out for the living God...and each other.

Each incarnation apart from our twin flame was spent either creating negative karma or balancing some of the karma that stood in the way of our reunion. At times we assumed various relationships with our twin flame—husband/wife, mother/son, father/daughter, and sister/brother—in order to unwind the negative strands of energy we had woven into our subconscious through our misuse of free will.

Now is the time, at the end of this cycle of history and moving into the Aquarian age, that people of light who are on a spiritual path need to learn to contact their twin flames. This search is prompted by our Higher Selves, but inadequately understood at the physical level. Often, when people learn that they share a unique mission with their twin flame, they begin to search physically for that one special soul instead of seeking their wholeness within. This is always a detour on the path to soul liberation. It is our relationship to God and our Higher Self that holds the key to finding and becoming one with our twin flame.

The Taj Mahal, built by the Mogul Emperor Shah Jahan as a tomb for his beloved wife, is a tribute to the majesty of divine love. It stands as a shrine to the eternal love of twin flames.

ALCHEMICAL MARRIAGE

*C*osmic law requires that we first define our own identity in God before we can completely unlock the joint spiritual potential of our twin flames. For until twin flames achieve a certain level of mastery and oneness with their own Real Selves, they are often unable to cope with the weight of their negative karma as it is amplified by the presence of their twin flame. The same unique factor that gives twin flames their great spiritual power—their identical blueprint of identity—can likewise cause the amplification of their negative patterns.

Ultimately each and every one of us must learn to change the negative patterns, the base metal of the human ego, into the gold of our divine or Real Self. This is called the alchemical marriage—the marriage of our soul, the feminine aspect of our being, to the 'Lamb' who is the real and enduring spiritual self, the masculine aspect. The love of this beloved Christ Self, i.e., that part of us who maintains constant contact with the Source —the I AM Presence—is an incomparable love. This is the Beloved for whom the saints of East and West have given their all.

By daily accelerating consciousness through their communion with God, the saints gradually transcended the human ego. Eventually their souls merged with their real spiritual self as they ascended back to the heart of God. "For this corruptible must put on incorruption, and this mortal must put on immortality." (I Cor. 15:53)

CREATION
OF TWIN FLAMES

(Fig. 1–2) *Representing the masculine and feminine polarity of God's wholeness, T'ai chi rotates and divides into two identical spheres—twin flames of the One. A drop from the ocean of God's being, each sphere, or Divine Monad, consists of the I AM Presence surrounded by the spheres (rings of color, of light) which make up the Causal Body. In this way, the Father-Mother God created us in their own image—male and female.*

FIG. 1

FIG. 2

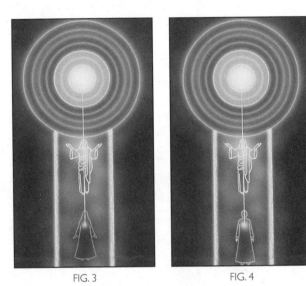

FIG. 3   FIG. 4

(Fig. 3–4) *Each I AM Presence then sends forth a ray—a soul. Each soul focuses the opposite polarity—one, masculine; the other, feminine. Between the soul evolving on earth and the I AM Presence stands the Christ Self—our personal mediator between Spirit and Matter. We may rise to become one with our Christ Self by exercising free will and achieving mastery on earth. This is the 'alchemical' marriage that must precede the eternal marriage of twin flames.*

46

(Fig. 5–6) *Adam and Eve symbolize the testing required by God of all twin flames. Although each of us came forth from Spirit to fulfill our mission to take dominion over the earth, we have fallen from the state of perfection (Eden) through our own disobedience and rebellion against cosmic law. As a result, we have had to endure the suffering of being separated from our twin flames for many incarnations as we endeavor to balance our karma.*

FIG. 5

FIG. 6

(Fig. 7) *As soon as twin flames misqualified the energy of God, they began to create negative karma—coils of energy that form layers of negativity and density in their auras separating them from their own I AM Presence and their twin flame.*

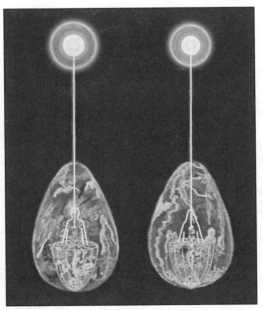

FIG. 7

(Fig. 8) *Through the daily use of the violet transmuting flame, this misqualified energy—such as resentment, irritation, anxiety, frustration—can be stripped of its negativity, purified, and returned to the seven rings of the Causal Body in the plane of Spirit as our "treasures stored in heaven."*

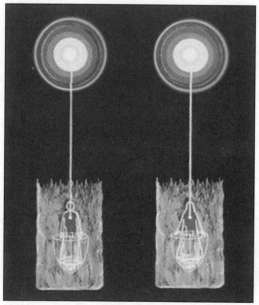

FIG. 8

(Fig. 9–10) *We can unite with our twin flame at inner levels, amplifying the threefold flame of God within our hearts, and using the dynamic polarity of our love to fulfill our mission. Our ultimate union occurs when we have become one with our I AM Presence and reunited in the plane of Spirit as immortal, God-free beings.*

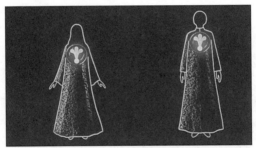

FIG. 9

FIG. 10

INNER CONTACT OF TWIN FLAMES

*Y*our twin flame may have already won soul liberation and reunited with God—or he may still be struggling to find the way. Where your twin flame is—what his or her state of consciousness is—can greatly influence your own ability to find wholeness. Because both of you share the same blueprint of identity— like the design of a snowflake, unique in all of cosmos—whatever energy you send forth is imprinted or stamped with that specific pattern. According to the law that like attracts like, all energy you release cycles to your twin flame—either hindering or helping him on the path to wholeness.

When you send forth love or hope, these qualities will uplift your twin flame. But if you are burdened with frustration or hatred, your twin flame will likewise feel the weight of these inharmonious feelings. Sometimes the inexplicable joys or depressions you feel are the moods of your other half registering on your own consciousness.

You can accelerate your spiritual progress if, in your prayer, meditation, or dynamic decrees,* you call to your I AM Presence for the inner heart contact with your twin flame. You can make the following invocation:

In the name of the Christ I call to the blessed I AM Presence of our twin flames for the sealing of our hearts as one for the victory of our mission to humanity. I invoke the light of the Holy Spirit for the consuming of all negative karma limiting the full expression of our divine identity and the fulfillment of our divine plan.

---

*Decrees are rhythmic prayers that call forth a powerful spiritual energy. This light-energy, combined with visualization, has the special quality of erasing and transmuting negative aspects of ourselves and enhancing positive aspects.

In saying this, even if you live in separate spheres, you can unite spiritually on higher planes and direct light into your own world and the world of your twin flame for the balancing of mutual karma. This inner contact magnifies the light and attainment you each have and releases the awesome power of the polarity of your love, enabling you to stand strong against the conflicts that inevitably come to the door of all who would defend love.

Inspired by the grandeur of love, artists, writers, and composers throughout the ages have expressed both love's exalted heights and tragic depths. In many of their masterpieces, we can sense an inner understanding of twin flames, their love for one another, and their encounters with karma and cosmic law.

Many famous operas can be interpreted

from this perspective. Even though some of the arias and duets give us a glimpse of the majestic love of twin flames, the plots often end in sorrow, tragedy, or death because one or both of the lovers fail a test of personal mastery—having not yet sealed their own individual path in God. These dramatic stories teach us of the pitfalls to be encountered in achieving the highest love and help us understand what *not* to do.

MADAME BUTTERFLY

*P*uccini's *Madame Butterfly* tells the story of the American Lieutenant Pinkerton and his contract marriage to Butterfly, a trusting fifteen-year-old Japanese girl. These two souls symbolize twin flames. Their Eastern and Western cultures represent both the masculine and feminine polarities of twin flames and the gulf that separates souls who have not yet balanced their karma and must endure the pain of separation as a result.

Pinkerton, a man hardened by the world, has lost the sense of the purity of true love. Although he is attracted by the beauty and charm of Butterfly, he deliberately plans to desert her for an American wife. In their brief time together, Pinkerton and his Japanese bride share intense moments of love—their souls uniting as one flame commemorating their original wholeness in God. And the fruit of this union is the conception of a child —a symbol of their great love.

But the Lieutenant does not realize she is carrying his child and is blinded by his own ambition, his cultural arrogance and selfish desires. He goes home to America, leaving Butterfly to trust in his eventual return. She waits patiently and hopefully, watching for his ship every day.

Pinkerton does return, several years later —with an American wife. In her grief at this desertion by her twin flame, Butterfly takes her life.

LOHENGRIN

*W*agner's opera *Lohengrin* illustrates the relationship of twin flames when the one who has ascended into Spirit endeavors to assist his beloved—still undergoing the tests and initiations on earth.

Elsa is falsely accused of murdering her brother, but she has absolute faith in the arrival of a knight in shining armor to save her. Lohengrin, Elsa's ascended twin flame, answers her inner call and descends from higher planes to rescue her. He glides across a lake in a boat pulled by a magical swan. He is a Grail Knight from the magical Grail Castle, a God-realized soul coming from another realm.

They are married, but Lohengrin, spiritual teacher to his twin flame, instructs Elsa that she may never ask his name. This is her great test of love—the same test Cupid required of Psyche in the classical myth of Cupid and Psyche. Neither Psyche nor Elsa could resist the temptation—both succumb to the human frailty of curiosity and discover the true identity of their lovers. Because of this disobedience, cosmic law requires their separation once again. Lohengrin returns to the plane of Spirit—there to await his twin flame's self-mastery and their ultimate reunion as does Cupid.

Literature abounds with famous lovers who may very well have been twin flames:

Dante finally reaching the point where Beatrice could present him to Christ, Penelope faithfully tending the flame of love that draws Ulysses home from his wanderings, Evangeline tirelessly searching for her beloved, Shakespeare pouring forth his love to the lady of the sonnets, Romeo and Juliet, Lancelot and Guenevere, Tristan and Isolde, Hiawatha and Minnehaha, Robert and Elizabeth Barrett Browning. All shared a love typical of twin flames.

SOUL MATES

Not all of the beautiful and soul-fulfilling loves are those of twin flames. There is also the love of very close, kindred souls called soul mates.

A soul mate is different from a twin flame. Soul mates come together because

As *Longfellow describes Hiawatha's* longing
for Minnehaha, he illustrates the dynamic polarity
of twin flames. "As unto the bow the cord is, So
unto the man is woman; Though she bends him,
she obeys him, Though she draws him, yet she
follows; Useless each without the other!"

they are working on mastering the same type of karma and developing the energies of the same chakra.* So soul mates have an attraction that is based on the sacred labor and on the path of self-mastery. A soul mate is like the echo of oneself in Matter working at the same task to fulfill a blueprint for God.

Mary and Joseph, the parents of Jesus, were soul mates sharing the responsibility for nurturing the Christ within their son. Both of their twin flames were in higher realms of light holding the balance for their mission. Many people today who are still balancing karma, but who are on the spiritual path, find themselves drawn to their soul mates for the fulfillment of a shared dharma or sacred labor.

---

*Chakras are spiritual centers within us that govern the flow of energy and represent different levels of consciousness.

KARMIC MARRIAGE

*B*esides twin flames and soul mates, a third kind of marriage relationship is frequently seen—the karmic marriage. Here, the two individuals are drawn together for the balancing of mutual karma. These marriages are often difficult but they are important in achieving mastery on the spiritual path. The husband and wife also gain the good karma of sponsoring and nurturing their children.

Some of these marriages may give the opportunity for the balancing of severe crimes of murder, betrayal, or extreme hatred. Very often the only way that we can overcome the record of that hatred is by the intense love expressed through the husband-wife relationship.

THE MARRIAGE UNION

$\mathcal{G}$od has blessed the human institution of marriage as an opportunity for two individuals to develop wholeness through the exchange of their Alpha-Omega polarities. Whether the union of twin flames, soul mates, or karmic partners, the marriage of man and woman is meant to be mystical, a commemoration of the soul's reunion with the beloved I AM Presence through the Christ, the blessed Mediator.

Jesus demonstrated the importance of marriage as an initiation on the Path when he chose to perform his first public miracle at the marriage feast of Cana—changing the water into wine. The essence of his message was that unless marriage is transformed by the Holy Spirit, it will only be an outer experience. It is our choice as to whether we are content with a marriage based on the water of the human consciousness or whether we desire a marriage based on the wine of the divine consciousness.

The cosmic interchange of divine love in the marriage relationship is meant to be the

same creative love that framed the universe in the beginning when God as Father gave forth the command, "Let there be light," and God as Mother answered, "And there was light." This creative flow can be expressed not only in physical union but also during cycles of dedicated celibacy as each partner goes within to commune with his beloved I AM Presence.

The exchange of the sacred energies in sexual union is for the transfer of spheres of cosmic consciousness—our Causal Bodies of light. The light energy resulting from this fusion enhances the positive qualities of each of the partners and strengthens their own divine identity—enabling them to carry their shared burden of karma. As the union is consecrated to the love of God, the harmonious blending of pure Father-Mother energies yields the Son, the Christ consciousness—whether it be in the form of a child, an inspiration, a successful enterprise, or a work of art.

When this exchange is not spiritualized through a recognition that God is both the lover and the beloved, the two individuals may experience physical pleasure, but they also unknowingly take on each other's karmic patterns without the benefit of a spiritually transmutative love. This may explain the frequent identity crises suffered by those who have intimate relationships on a casual basis; they take on so many karmic identities, effectively neutralizing their own, that they no longer know who they really are.

THE CIRCLE OF ONENESS

*H*ere is a ritual you can use to consecrate your sacred union with your partner and to seal your interchanges in the purity of God's love. You can also use this ritual to celebrate your oneness with your twin flame and with God.

Stand (alone or with your partner) and face the Chart of Your Divine Self* as you make your inner attunement with the star of your divinity, your I AM Presence. Meditate upon the sacred flame that burns within your heart. Visualize the arc of your love ascending from your heart to the heart of your I AM Presence. Take your right hand and dip it into the fires of your heart and draw the circle of oneness around yourselves (you and your partner, your twin flame or your I AM

*See p. 136 and note on p. 145.

Presence) as you stand in adoration of the One. Visualize this circle, twelve feet in diameter, as a line of sacred fire that will repel all that opposes your union.

See yourselves focusing the plus and minus of cosmic energies, two halves of the whirling T'ai Chi. Consecrate your love to your soul's reunion with the I AM Presence and to the ultimate reunion of you and your twin flame within the hallowed circle of God. As an additional protection of your oneness invoke the cherubim daily, for they are the guardians of love.

A vital mission awaits those whose energies are in harmony with divine love. I have seen twin flames whose love was never abated, who could hold the balance for an entire city and whose daily invocations could transmute hatred and crime and murder, holding that inner balance.

This is a high and holy calling. It's not for the mundane who desire the pleasure cult and its sensuality. This is the real inner path for those who understand that there is a cosmos aborning within us, that there's a world

Only after Dante has passed through the Inferno and Purgatorio for the expiation of his sins, does he experience the divine love of the Paradiso with his true love, Beatrice. Here she presents Dante to Christ.

to be saved, that millions of souls need our love, and that it can never be a selfish love.

In the cynicism of our age, however, many have lost the sense of the power of pure love. Few seem to have the buoyant, joyous attitude toward life where each day is a new opportunity to give our love as a unique gift to those around us. Too often we underestimate our ability to transform lives through our example.

Djwal Kul, known throughout the world as the Master D.K., once related this story of the miller and his wife.

There lived by the sea a gentle soul who was a miller. He and his wife served together to grind the grain for the people of their town. And it came to pass that in all the land there were no communities where so much happiness reigned as there. Their countrymen marveled and wondered, for they recognized that something unusual must have happened to make the members of this community so singularly wise and happy. And although the townsfolk themselves were born, grew up, matured to adulthood and passed from the screen of life within the community, never in all of their living were they able to understand the mystery.

Tonight I shall draw aside the curtain and tell you what made the people of this community so happy and prosperous, so joyous and wise.

It was the service of the miller and his wife and the love which they put into the flour. For this love was carried home in sacks of flour on the backs of those who patronized their mill and was then baked into their bread. At every meal the regenerative power of love from the miller and his wife was radiated around the table and it entered their physical bodies as they partook of the bread. Thus, like radioactive power, the energy of this vibrant love from the miller and his wife was spread throughout the community.

The neighbors did not know the reason of their happiness and none of the people were ever able to discover it. For sometimes—although they live side by side—mankind are unable to pry the most simple secrets about one another.

AQUARIAN AGE ALCHEMY

*E*ven as the miller and his wife silently communicated their love to others, you and your twin flame or partner also influence countless lives around you through your "radioactive" thoughts, feelings, and actions. You have an opportunity to assist life or to place a burden upon it—either by interacting with the negative energy of your past karma cycling to the surface of your consciousness or by recognizing this energy as a challenge to your harmony and love and transmuting it.

The key to transmuting or changing past karma and fulfilling your mission with your twin flame is the violet flame, a spiritual energy given by God to man for his acceleration into the Aquarian age.* This action of the Holy Spirit transforms negative energy—anger into love, irritation into peace, suspicion into trust—so that you can influence life positively as you work toward your ultimate victory on the spiritual path.

When you visualize this violet flame and call it forth into your consciousness, it instantaneously begins to change negative energy patterns accumulated over thousands of lifetimes. You begin to experience feelings

---

*The two-thousand-year period that will follow the age of Pisces, which was inaugurated by the birth of Jesus Christ.

of joy, lightness and hope. It's as if your entire consciousness were being dipped into a chemical solution of purple liquid which dissolves the karma of centuries.

This is the dispensation many people have been waiting for. This is why we've been evolving these tens of thousands of years, why we have gone through the cycles of understanding God as the Father and God as the Son. Now we are coming to the Holy Spirit energy, the sacred science of alchemy, of self-transformation—through the violet flame.

A simple but powerful violet-flame mantra you can give is: "I AM a being of violet fire, I AM the purity God desires." "I AM" is the affirmation of the God within, the I AM Presence—the same Presence who declared to Moses "I AM THAT I AM. . . . This is my name for ever, and this is my memorial unto all generations." (Exod. 3:14–15) Daily immersing ourselves in the cleansing energy of the violet flame through reciting violet flame mantras is the quickest and most effective way to maintain our harmony and accelerate our consciousness for our ultimate reunion with God and our twin flame. (See p. 148 for more violet flame mantras.)

This is the baptism of the Holy Ghost that was prophesied in the New Testament by John the Baptist (Matt. 3:11). This is the gift of God for the Aquarian age. This is how the days are shortened for the elect—for the homeward journey, the overcoming of the round of the wheel of rebirth.

YEARNING FOR WHOLENESS

*T*he oncoming Aquarian age is an age for the understanding of God's energy in polarity as the masculine and feminine principles of the universe. How we experience that energy as our true identity, how we understand it as the essence of twin flames, and how we use it as the integrative power of divine love for the betterment of mankind will determine whether or not we survive as individuals and, ultimately, as a human race.

You may be reading this book right now because the only thing that stands between you and your twin flame is a layer of negative energy just waiting to be consumed by the joyous, bubbling action of the violet flame.

Your mission, your twin flame, and your ultimate reunion in the heart of God await you!

Mark and Elizabeth Prophet, c. 1972

LOVE, MARRIAGE, AND BEYOND:
WHAT I HAVE LEARNED

RECOGNIZING YOUR
TWIN FLAME

*F*irst of all, I never knew that there was any such thing as a twin flame until, at eighteen, I read an obscure book about soul mates.

My quest, however, in those early years of searching which had been going on since childhood, was to find God and to discover what his mission was for me. I was very determined to get to the foundation of my life and to do what I knew I had to do. It was an impelling call from within.

In retrospect I have seen that in searching for God, I used to leave my body in sleep at night, go to the inner temples and work with the Ascended Masters and with Mark—who was about twenty years my senior according to the calculations of this life.*

As far as twin flames are concerned, the age of the body has nothing to do with the age of the soul, because the souls are the same age, having begun together in the beginning in the 'white fire body' of the Divine Whole.

And so, with the encounter on inner planes as prologue, we met when I was twenty-two and he was forty-two. I was looking for the Teacher and the Guru because I knew that somewhere there was that one

---

*Out-of-the-body soul experiences in the 'etheric' retreats of the Ascended Masters are the ongoing method of soul advancement provided by God for earth's evolutions. The Ascended Masters are enlightened spiritual beings who once lived on earth, fulfilled their reason for being, and have ascended (reunited with God).

who was going to give to me the key to my mission. What I did not know was that my inner understanding included the awareness that my Teacher would be my twin flame.

So, when I saw Mark Prophet for the first time, I recognized him as Teacher. He, seeing me for the first time, recognized me as twin flame.

It was a very interesting experience. I was so one-pointed in the direction of finding the Teacher and so elated to have found the One, that I was almost burdened by having to deal with another relationship at the same time.

I wanted to be absolutely certain, and I wanted to have the confirmation in my own being, that every step I took was right and was the will of God so that I would not make any mistake to the harm of any part of life. And so I asked God to reveal to me and confirm within my own being that this indeed was my twin flame.

Weeks later I had a very astounding experience. It was one of those indelible experiences that never dims with time. I happened to look into a mirror where I was dressing. And I looked up, and I did not see myself—I saw the face of Mark Prophet.

Now, if you can ever imagine looking in a mirror and not seeing yourself, it's a very shocking experience.

What I saw was really the revelation of the inner soul pattern, not just of the soul, which is that potential to become God, but I saw the image of the 'man behind the man'. It was as if I was seeing the archetypal likeness of myself in the masculine polarity.

I drew close to examine it in greater detail. It did not fade but 'waited' for me to take in every line of it. It was ancient. It had always been. It was sculpted in marble, etched in crystal, yet 'flesh of my flesh'. I saw that I was the reflection in the negative (feminine) polarity of that positive (masculine) image.

When my being had registered the confirmation of the inner pattern, his face was no longer in the mirror but fully awakened in my soul.

It was awesome to contemplate the meaning of the twin flame—to have felt the inner reality and now to understand how the twin flame could actually be oneself— the other half, the 'divine alter ego' (to grasp at a definition), like the person you are on the other side of yourself.

This awareness precedes love. It is the mystery of Life itself that one must enter before one loves. One isn't quite ready to love—one has a lot to think about. And I thought—and thought:

It was undeniable—the inescapable truth.

There was no turning back. The die had been cast beyond time and space. It was mine to choose to act upon a preordained Reality. Or to walk away from it—but how? It would always be with me. He was myself, as he had told me.

I had called to God for my Teacher and he had sent me my twin flame. Now we must sort out our lives and chart our course.

This inner knowing—this certain knowledge of the soul—has nothing to do with being in love in the human sense of the word.

I wish to clarify this point because for as long as I have been teaching, during the last thirty-seven years since this experience, I have received hundreds of letters from people concerning twin flames. They tell me that they have found their twin flame and they base it on a human love experience, compatible personalities and astrology, or outer indexes that point more to the soul mate relationship or the karmic polarization than to the inner reality of twin flames.

Although these may provide an indication of compatibility, they do not necessarily confirm the depth of soul oneness that we find when we go to the bedrock of being where the truth of our twin flame can be known.

Remember that Paul said, "Flesh and blood cannot inherit the kingdom of God." (I Cor. 15:50) We are not twin flames by virtue of the condition of our flesh and blood, our personality, our astrology, our karma, or our mutual attraction. We are twin flames by our origin in the same sphere of being called the white fire body. Only we two came out of that One—only we share the unique divine design—"male and female" (Gen. 1:27), Elohim created us. And no other will ever share the same identical pattern.

If the twin flame relationship is not going to serve a spiritual purpose—if its reestablishment in this life is going to mean the breaking up of families and homes, if it's going to cause a cataclysm in people's lives because they are in different situations that they are bound to be involved with (because they are resolving past karma)—then often the outer mind would rather not deal with what the soul knows at the subconscious level. And so the outer mind does not readily admit to the 'pre-cognition' that is ever-present with the soul.

For instance, I have seen twin flames where the man was twenty and the woman was seventy. And their meeting did not produce instant love and marriage. Nor did the relationship become anything more than a loyal friendship and a mutual fondness. In fact, though inseparable, they never even realized they were twin flames.

It wasn't necessary for them to know. Their souls knew, and they accomplished what they were supposed to without having to deal with any more than they were ready for.

KARMA IN RELATIONSHIPS

*T*he encounter that produces a spiritual polarity and an intense mutual love can be the result of many different circumstances. The twin flame tie is one. Soul mates is another. And then there is karma. The karmic tie may be the tightest of all. Because it is not free, it is binding. Because it is not balanced, the internal harmonies are wanting. And from time to time, there is an emptiness, a loneliness, that reveals the inadequacy of a relationship based solely on karma. This, too, shall pass.

We may have several such relationships with people with whom we have made karma in our past lives—good karma and bad karma. Sometimes the worse the karma, the more intense the impact when we first meet someone, because this is God—the God* we ourselves have imprisoned through past negative activity—and we run to greet that one to set him (her) free from our own past transgressions of his (her) being. And we love much because there is much to be forgiven.

A negative experience of the past—such as violence, passionate hatred, murder, noncaring for one's children, one's family, something that you have been involved in with someone else that has caused an imbalance both in their soul and in yours and perhaps in the lives of many—is experienced as a

---

*Everyone is in reality a manifestation of God and we meet God face to face in every part of life.

weight upon the heart and an absence of resolution at the soul level. This is a very gnawing condition that troubles our consciousness until it is resolved by love.

Your soul knows why you have come into embodiment. You have been told by your spiritual teachers, your Christ Self, or guardian angel: "There is this situation with so-and-so that requires resolution. You and this person, by your neglect, by your failure to act, once caused the collapse of this city. Or because you walked away from your responsibility many people were involved in a famine."

These are not unlikely situations. The ramifications of what we do by committing sin or by refusing to serve life are very great, and they're very heavy. At inner levels the soul who is on the Homeward path (going home to the Father-Mother God) is very conscientious and desirous of righting the wrongs of the past—because she knows that righting the wrongs of lifetimes of ignorant and erroneous sowings is the only way to get back to the heavenly place we started from.

On the bright side, a Master may have told you before you took embodiment in this life that because of the many constructive labors for humanity you have done together, you are assigned an even greater responsibility with this person in this life. And because of your good karma, you will be happy and fruitful and have many victories for the right.

In this century of our souls' acceleration toward Aquarius you may experience more than one relationship of both kinds. We are winding up the loose ends of our karma with a number of people in this cycle of history.

These equations of our karma can cause distress, divorce, soul-searching, and a real need to understand why our lives have not followed the perfect storybook version. The knowledge of karma and reincarnation can teach us a lot about the bumpy road of relationships, some beautiful and some very unpleasant—but all very necessary to the soul's evolution and the path of defining our true selfhood with God, Christ, and our twin flame.

So you may meet someone—and this may occur in the latter teen-age years and the twenties or anytime—and the impact will be stunning. It's like the impact of planetary bodies. It will be stunning because at the subconscious level you are so elated that you have found the person with whom you can balance a certain record of karma.

Your soul knows that if you do not get through that karma, you cannot go on to the next slice of the spiral of life and then on to world service and the creative projects you want most to do with the one you love most—

even though you may have never met.

This sense of obligation translates as a need to give of oneself and to receive, the desire to love and be loved, because the flame of love is the all-consuming fire of God that dissolves the records of non-love or anti-love as we give and take in a relationship.

There may be children involved, and you may have agreed to bring into the world a certain number of children who are a part of a certain family or group karma. Because the goal of life is reunion with the Christ Self, reunion with your I AM Presence, and ultimately the spiritual reunion with your twin flame, you realize that if you don't get this karma balanced, you will not get to your perfect love.

So, the faster you submit to the law of your own karma—which is in fact the law of love—the faster both you and your partner are going to be liberated for the next step in your divine plan.

We are reaping what we have sown, but through service to each other we can accelerate karmic cycles.

You may have one of these very intense interchanges in a relationship. You may be in the tight coil of that karma, and you may be aware of just what the causes were that set in motion the effects you are seeing pass before you and between you every day—or you may be blissfully unaware of anything but love.

You're in the pink. There is nothing more important. There's no one in all the world you'd rather be with. There's nothing you'd rather do. The love is there. The newness of the relationship is there. You marry, you start a family, you start working together, and you start working out this karma.

Well, you all know the expression "the

honeymoon is over." That expression has to do with the impact of karma once there is a binding relationship of marriage. This is why some people just don't want to get married—because they have a resistance to "bearing one another's burden."

They simply don't want the responsibility. They say marriage would ruin everything, but what they mean is taking on each other's karma would really mess things up. Each half of the partnership is still too self-centered to give up that independence which can be kept only if they don't pick up each other's karmic load.*

---

*Living with someone or having an affair is another story entirely. We may share our karma for awhile and pool our resources for a worthwhile or enjoyable experience, but when we go our separate ways, we go back on the way of our separate karma without having really balanced our karma at the depth of mutual burden-bearing that true spiritual progress requires. The more casual the relationship and the less serious the commitment, the easier it is to walk away when the very first head-on encounter with karma takes place.

But that is precisely the inner meaning of the ritual of marriage—that we love so much, *so very much* that we eagerly share and bear the karma of our spouse with our own. We want to be one at all levels of consciousness.

MARRIAGE

*T*he marriage vow reflects this commitment of souls who plight their troth: "...to have and to hold from this day forward, for better, for worse, for richer, for poorer, in sickness and in health, to love and to cherish till death us do part." It is this totality of oneness spiritually, karmically, and in all ways that Jesus described when he said, "and they twain shall be one flesh." (Matt. 19:5)

If marriage were a mere physical union, divorce, when it occurs, would not be so emotionally devastating. Divorce is a surgery of pulling apart the two that have become one; and all the battles about who owns what and who gets the children really center around the excruciating process of redefining one's self apart from the 'other self'.

Taking the marriage vow signifies that

when we take one another "to my wedded wife/to my wedded husband," we will stand together, come what may, in the other's life and karma. Since the future and the subconscious are not known on the wedding day, and the vow is so "final," it is the most serious and far-reaching contract we will ever sign in our lifetime. That's why St. Paul warned us not to be unequally yoked together with those of unlike mind, and recommended we consider "what communion hath light with darkness?" (II Cor. 6:14) in interpersonal relationships.

If you marry someone who has less attainment on the spiritual path or a heavier karma than yours, then, when the honeymoon is over, you're going to feel the weight. You will know that you have taken on the karma of someone else, and that someone else is on the good end of the bargain because he or she's gotten all your light, your talent, or your money. But you may want it that way—because you love so much and you want to give yourself to that person, or to the God in that person.

It may be the correct decision. It may be ordained by your karma that you must lay down your life for this old friend because he once saved you from utter loss and despair. It may be the correct decision even if it later appears as a mistake or the worst of all possible choices. You made the decision because you needed to make the decision—because your soul had a need to resolve.

You may have only needed to learn the whys and wherefores of factors of decision-making in your own personal psychology— or to face a part of him (or her) that is really a part of yourself that must be worked through and overcome. This could be a part of yourself you were never willing to admit was there until you were forced to confront it in the personality of another.

Don't get upset with yourself when you find out these things. It's all part of the Plan. God loves you and he wants you to come home to his heart whole—psychologically, spiritually, and karmically whole. And he is giving you these varied experiences and encounters so that you will be weaned from unreality, love him more than all of these, and see Christ's face smiling at you just beyond the veil of the one you are loving.

This need for resolution can be understood with an analogy. It's the way an oyster feels when he gets a little grain of sand in his shell, and he's got to keep on covering it over because it's a botheration, it's an irritant to his world. Because he wants resolution, he makes a pearl out of it.

Well, that's how karma is. It irritates. And we want to smooth it over. We want to make it right.

Now, the thing about this karmic marriage or relationship that you are into is that you can never get out of it, you can never get free of it if you don't fulfill every jot and tittle of the law—the law of karma that compels the highest expression of love in order to be free. If you don't balance ultimately and finally what there is between you, you will reembody and you will still have to enter into some sort of a relationship with that person, even if it is a business partnership.

DIVORCE

No one in heaven or on earth can separate you from your twin flame. That's why Jesus said, "What therefore God hath joined together, let not man put asunder." (Matt. 19:6)

When you come before the altar to be married, you are receiving a blessing *by your choice,* by your freewill decision, but this marriage may or may not be a condition or an estate where it can be said, "whom God hath joined together." Marriages are made on earth by two people for various reasons; as such they are not necessarily *the* marriage that was made in heaven.

God created you and your twin flame out of the same white fire body in the beginning. The story of Eve being formed out of the rib taken from Adam is an attempt to illustrate this mystical origin. Because of this oneness in the nucleus of divine selfhood, in all other conditions and circumstances of life, no one can separate you from that love of God in your twin flame. That is the real meaning of that passage of Scripture.

So, karmic marriages and other conditions of life may come and go, and they are for a purpose. So long as the karma remains (unless there be alternative means for working it out), they are binding. While we are in the midst of them, we can make of these marriages a celebration on earth of our inner union with our twin flame. This is lawful.

What is *not* lawful is that you treat such a relationship halfheartedly or even resentfully and do not give it your best and the most fervent love of your heart because you say, "Well, this person is not my twin flame. And this is just a karmic situation, so I'll give it a token effort and bide my time until the real thing comes along." Well, that's a very good way to prolong the resolution of your karma and to make more karma.

We look at life with the understanding that whoever we are dealing with *is God*.

The person is God—in manifestation. The divine flame is God. The potential is God. And we must love that person with our whole heart, with the purest and highest love that we would have for God and for our twin flame.

That love is liberating. It is a transmutative force. We need forgiveness in relationships. We need liberally to forgive others and to forgive ourselves because that's the whole point of karma. We all have much to forgive and much to be forgiven for, or we would not find ourselves on this planet at this point in time and space.

So it doesn't matter if you're married to your twin flame or if you've ever met your twin flame. What matters is that you realize the sacredness of marriage and the relationship of man and woman, and that this polarity is always representative of 'Alpha and

Omega'—the Masculine/Feminine Co-Creators of Life in the white fire body of the Godhead depicted by the Chinese as the T'ai Chi.

YOUR UNION IN ETERNITY

*W*herever your twin flame is, even if your twin flame is a cosmic being, your twin flame needs your support and your love. Because, if you are in a negative vibration, you can actually hinder the activity and service of an Ascended Master, an angel, or someone in embodiment who is trying to fight for freedom, someone in China who's taking a stand against oppression or lying in a psychiatric hospital being injected with drugs to make him a vegetable.

Whoever your twin flame is, if you let down your light, your self-discipline, or your love with those friends and family ties you now have, you are letting down first, Almighty God, and second, your twin flame. And ultimately you will suffer, because a setback to your twin flame is a setback to you.

On that day when you make your ascension back to the heart of God and you would like to know your twin flame is going to ascend also, that twin flame may not be ready to ascend. He or she may have another thousand years to embody upon earth, because you did not supply that extra thrust of spirituality and light and selflessness that could have propelled that person into a higher dimension of their own consciousness. (I don't recommend that you blame yourself for anything or everything that has or can go wrong in life, but I do ask that you consider how much more you can do for yourself and others to make things go right.)

So when we say, "no man is an island, no woman is an island," we understand that the twin flame, as the other half of the whole, is experiencing the ramifications and the repercussions of our life. This knowledge makes life worth doing and doing well. Sharing love and serving others' needs and helping them grow is all a part of giving yourself in advance to that perfect love that will be there when you're both ready—really ready.

I also understand that it is lawful in the Aquarian age for the ritual of marriage to be celebrated for other reasons than the marriage of twin flames, because the laws of God take into account and accommodate the human condition.

We all have a human condition right now. You have a scroll upon which is written the law of your life, which is the law of your karma. As a co-creator with God, you have made good karma, you have made bad karma.

The law of the inner blueprint is written underneath this page. Our human karma is like an overlay, which we've put over the original fiery blueprint. We see that overlay, and we see, peeking through, what is underneath.

We all know how life should be for us, how we would like it to be in the idyllic, Edenic, sense of the word. Then we look about us, and we are still in the state of toiling. But we have hope in our heart: Christ is the hope of our glory in God and in our twin flame. The hope lies in the fact that we know what is real at inner levels.

We know where we have come from. We know who we are. We know where we are going. Through the Holy Spirit, God has given to us the gift of the violet flame to get there. So we take every day as an opportunity to erase the overlay, so that one day that entire page can be turned over, and once again we are returned to that point of Eden and the bliss of Love in the hallowed circle of our Oneness.

THE WEIGHT OF KARMA

We know that most of the sacred scriptures of the world contain a story about man and woman and their fall. This actually refers to the descent of you and your twin flame from the etheric octave—the place of the pristine purity of the golden-age consciousness—to the place where we are now, weighted down by the world karma that is upon us.

It is a weight of untransmuted energy, and it begins to interfere with the untrammeled and free flow of light in the heart and the chakras, so they are no longer spinning at such an intense velocity of light. We are literally earthbound.

We know the meaning of the weight of a physical body. We can all do only so much in each given day, and then the body is spent, and we must put it to rest and recharge it again.

So that descent is the point of sorrow. The greatest sorrow, of course, is separation from the face-to-face encounter with the beloved I AM Presence, the face-to-face encounter with the Person of Christ, our Christ Self, or the embodied Teacher, and then the loss of the perpetual communion with the twin flame.

At that point, we begin to make karma with others, and there are the long separations which may go on for many lifetimes. This is sometimes the source of depression and a sense of nonfulfillment in life.

Often, of course, it is an illusion, because people say, "Well, if only my twin flame were here, everything would be wonderful. I can't get along with this person. We're not really alike. We don't agree. We don't think alike" —all these problems that come up in relationships.

We have the sense of the ideal, the sense of who this person is, and we believe that this person will absolutely, completely, and totally be our complement, and all of our dreams and wishes will come true.

Well, it just isn't so. If you can't get along with yourself, you won't get along with your twin flame or soul mate. Actually, twin flames develop different personalities by being separated for so long. They go through negative conditionings by negative experiences. Twin flames in embodiment are not necessarily alike. They may have an astrology that clashes.

I remember an astrologer once told Mark and me that we should never be married because we couldn't possibly get along with the astrology that we had. He was a Capricorn and I'm an Aries, which is a combination of an earth and fire sign. They say either the earth will put out the fire or the fire will scorch the earth. But I say, Love conquers all.

WORKING ON
RELATIONSHIPS

*W*ell, I realized that there was only one way that my relationship with Mark would work, and that was that one of us had to take the lead. Mark was supremely qualified to be the leader because he was the Teacher of my soul.

I understood completely who was who in that relationship. And if I didn't understand it, I was very swiftly reminded by Mark! So, luckily, I figured that one out, and we lived happily ever after.

I was very happy to be in the role of disciple to Mark. He represented the Master to me as no other could. He was the only person who could have brought me to the very quintessence of my own being and simultaneously to the submission unto Christ. He knew my soul as no one else could. He bore to me the love of the universe. To be near him was and is to be enveloped in God.

He knew me in the beginning. He knew what I should be manifesting and what I was not. He knew what was excess human consciousness picked up as baggage in life from all my many interactions with so many people and conditions.

Thus Mark was highly qualified to bring me to an abrupt waking awareness of this disparity between the inner divine being that I AM, and you are, and all of us are, and sometimes the paltry and shameful manifestation—which is shameful not because it's so "bad," but it's shameful because it's such a mediocre version of what the inner Self really is.

When you have a masterful one such as Mark who can plug you back into the power of that original design, you are electrified with the sense within you of who you really are and what you should be. Mark Prophet galvanized my life for Christ and revealed Christ as the Saviour and Bridegroom of my soul.

Your Real Self, your Holy Christ Self, and the Holy Christ Self of your twin flame is the magnet that will draw you and your twin flame together—in this world and the next. "And I," to paraphrase Jesus, "if the I AM in me be lifted up, then I will draw my twin flame unto me."

So, we have to go back to the statement of Paul once again, that "flesh and blood cannot inherit the kingdom of God." (I Cor. 15:50) And flesh and blood does not guarantee you a harmonious relationship with anyone, including your twin flame. What will guarantee it is your determination to work hard at a relationship.

There is no relationship—any friendship, our children, brothers and sisters, relatives, professional relationships—which, if it's going to endure, does not require work. We all have to give of ourselves and give a lot in order to sustain that interaction with anyone.

So you have to see that twin flames, by having gone all over the earth in all kinds of incarnations and circumstances, might, through karmic conditions, have superficial personality clashes. When these are seen as superficial and we get to the heart of the matter, then we're in the driver's seat, and we become co-creators with God.

You see, twin flames do make karma with each other in various embodiments, and that karma also has to be balanced when they finally get back together. So there can be a tremendous sense of injustice between twin flames.

That explains what occurs in karmic marriages where people are constantly fighting and you can see no purpose to the relationship. So you say, "Why don't they just quit and separate, because this has been going on for years." And next thing you know they're back as lovebirds, starting all over again. This repeats and repeats and repeats. And nobody can understand what's going on except the two people involved.

Of course, it's a very dangerous thing because there's a lot of karma-making in those heavy scenes. Ultimately, they may become so self-destructive that often the solution is for people to go their separate ways, *even if they are twin flames, and even if they haven't balanced their mutual karma.*

I've known of twin flames who have destroyed their lives and their marriages, when if they had just had an understanding of the law of love, where love begets love, and a commitment to the relationship, they could have made some progress.

I've seen twin flames who are alcoholics, drug addicts. I've seen them ruin their lives and their children's lives and wind up in the dregs of disappointment. And life comes to a conclusion and they pass from the screen of life and they are sorry beyond words at the soul level when they see that they utterly failed in their assignment to go down into physical embodiment and get things together and make things happen.

GETTING READY FOR YOUR TWIN FLAME

So you need to be ready to meet your twin flame. You need to have a good deal of self-control. You've got to love Love enough to respect it, to hold your peace and your harmony when those old records of ancient clashes come up for resolution. You've got to hold on to your Dream, seal those unkind words, the cruel criticism, the put-down, and anything that will shatter the matrix of the most beautiful gift Life will ever give to you—perfect love.

Give in. You don't have to win every argument. Preserve the integrity and self-respect of the one you love and thereby guarantee your own. The mantra of John the Baptist will go a long way on the path of sacrifice and surrender that marriage is:

"He must increase, but I must decrease."
(John 3:30)

So you have to have a dedication to something more than your twin flame, and that something more is God. You've got to love God first and be very sure of your path and your service and that you're not going to give in to discord or the theatrics of the human ego and all kinds of self-indulgences and demands—whether your own or your mate's.

You cannot demand that anyone be a complement to your human personality with all of its faults. You cannot expect someone to be to you father and mother, brother and sister, lover, husband or wife, and son and daughter all at once, so that every time you experience the least little bit of a problem, your idea is that this twin flame or this spouse is going to move right in and pick you up and everything's going to be rosy.

You have to decide to be complete in yourself—stop that pouting and self-pity and that constant demand for attention—and then by the magnet of your wholeness, you will attract wholeness in another person.

Read I Corinthians 13 often and keep a copy of the Prayer of Saint Francis of Assisi on your nightstand so you remember that true love is self-givingness. *The Prophet* by Kahlil Gibran will restore your memory of the bliss of love and marriage. True love is sacrificial—*always* putting the beloved first.

Now, I have to tell you that sometimes and in some circumstances, because of such a difference between twin flames, God actually works it so that they embody as brother and sister, or as father and child, or as members of the same sex. This is because a marriage relationship would not be profitable and more than likely, based on the record of past performance, would hinder more than help their soul evolution.

There is nothing more painful to a cosmos than an argument between twin flames, because it is from strife in that circle of Oneness that war and every other desolation ensue. It violates the Father-Mother God in heaven and on earth.

If you ever remember as a child hearing an argument between your father and mother, you know that you could have no worse experience. It's a crushing blow to every part of life that those who hold the office of Father and Mother should experience any discord in the flow of that divine love.

It is painful to the souls of twin flames as well. At inner levels, we ourselves don't want this to occur, because we know how damaging it is. We know it will keep us separated for succeeding incarnations. We have to give. There is no other way.

We all have human weaknesses. We all have human problems. We have human things we haven't overcome. When we think of the spouse, made in the image of the Divine Spouse, the one who would be the perfect one for us, we always imagine that that person should be perfect.

So when they're not perfect in our eyes, which measurement we take by our own state of imperfection, we throw a tantrum. We rant, we rave, we make demands, we scream, we sob. All these things are going on in marriages all over the world because somebody is expecting another person to be something more than that person is and better than they themselves are. If we have faults, we want the other person to be perfect.

So we make demands of people in a

marriage that are totally unrealistic. And this is why marriages fall apart. Not to mention, of course, that one of the basic reasons people marry is for sensual gratification. Putting that aside, all of the other psychological situations of strident tensions between human personalities become a horrendous mark against the divine image of Father-Mother God—against wholeness.

I advocate that you meditate upon your Self and your life in both the divine and the human sense of the word and realize that if you want to attract the beautiful lady of grace or the knight in shining armor, you have to *become* that counterpart first. Look at yourself in terms of scrubbing up that karma with violet flame and meditation and coming to a resolution of your own psychology.

In seeking your twin flame, the only real

desire that you ought to have is to bring to that twin flame the gift of your love, your self, your own spiritual attainment as well as your outer professional accomplishments.

What bouquet of flowers are you ready to bring to your twin flame today?

I'd like you to meditate upon this because it's a most important part of your under-standing of your psychology. After you've defined what you are capable of giving on one piece of paper, you should write down what you know, by past performance and present awareness, you're not capable of giving.

You might say, "Well, one thing I can't do: I don't know how to cook. So I can't cook a meal for this twin flame." Whether you're a man or a woman, you like to have somebody cook a meal for you once in a while. So you ought to learn to cook.

Get down to the basics in life. Can you

keep a schedule? Can you add happiness to a household? Can you be patient with children? Can you be patient with the child in the person that you're imagining is going to come down the highway one of these days?

Look at how you interact with yourself. Can you get along with yourself or do you have problems with yourself? Do you have moods? Do you have ups and downs?

Now, when you look at the balance between the flowers you can offer and the weeds you have not yet plucked from your garden or the barren earth where you haven't planted a flower, then you turn around and you get on the receiving end.

Pretend you're the other person. You're the other person seeing you coming down the road. Are they going to be interested? Is this wonderful person that you're imagining going to want you? If they're so wonderful, they may be *so* wonderful that they may be *too* wonderful! They may not even notice you!

In other words, you've got to become very wonderful yourself, as wonderful as the person that you desire to be with. And you have to be that in fact and in reality and not in fantasy.

So now the other person is coming down the road. Maybe it is your twin flame and they see you—you're standing there—and they walk on by. You say, "Wait a minute. You're supposed to stop when you get to me!"

But they didn't stop when they got to you because they didn't find in you a magnet. You didn't have the capacity to magnetize the person that you imagine is your divine polarity.

Well, why didn't you have the capacity? You have to imagine what that person would be looking for. You know what you want in that person. You know the virtues and qualities. If you don't contain the same virtues and qualities you're looking for, the person will not recognize you. It'll be like strangers in a crowded room who never speak.

Many people think it's all in the package, in the appearance. But it isn't. That wears away very quickly. You've got to have heart. You've got to have soul. You've got to be willing to give. You've also got to be willing to demonstrate that you do have the qualifications for the job.

What's the job? It's an office. It's saying, "Here's the person who is the 'Alpha'. Here's the person who's the 'Omega'. I want to be the counterpart to that person. I have to be able to prove to that person that I can hold the balance for their mission. I can uphold them. I can serve with them. I can provide the counterpart of qualities they need." Whatever they do, you've got to be able to give something to their life that they need, because all relationships are based on need.

You have to be very honest in a relationship, because you may see well in advance that you're not going to be able to provide a major aspect that that person needs, and you may see they're not going to be able to provide yours. If you're the one that can see it, then you will bear the karma of going into that relationship because your human self wants it even though your heart and your mind and your soul really know that it's not going to work.

The reason that this is such a situation of concern to us all is that each of us really does have a fundamental need to relate to at least one person in life in a very personal way.

So when we recognize the fundamental soul need in life for "the Friend," we need to be careful to understand what it is that we really need in that friend. A friend that does not meet that need, a friend that we can't give and take with, who is of a different vibration than what our soul requires, becomes no friend at all—in fact, he or she becomes a shackle and a drag.

When we have such a relationship with someone, we realize we're wasting our life and their life. We've only got threescore and ten and maybe a little bit more. And we've got things we've got to do.

FINDING
WHOLENESS

Sublimation is one way of dealing with the absence, in physical proximity, of the friend. It means taking the energy of the need and the creative force of our life itself and projecting it into the future as a future goal. In the meantime, while reaching out to that goal of the perfect love, we love all life. We love people, many people, individually and personally, in a very deep way. We have good relationships, good associates.

But we understand that what we are looking for and what we know is there, just beyond the veil, already exists. In the process of our self-mastery, we learn to live with that fact, and we say, "I will go through the coil of experience. I will accept no substitute and no diversion from my goal." It's like knowing you're going to meet someone in Rome, and you realize that it takes a certain amount of time to travel there.

If we don't understand sublimation, or 'etherealization', if we are a creature of wants and demands—"I want what I want and I want it now and it *has* to be now"—we will accept a lesser standard in our lives. And we will actually not have the power to attract to ourselves what really is the fulfillment of the divine meeting as well as the divine plan for this embodiment.

So, it's all right to acknowledge the need. But remember, a need is also an absence of wholeness, and an absence of wholeness makes you incomplete. When you're incomplete, you are not focusing on the divine magnet of wholeness that can attract to you the very thing you need to complete your wholeness.

A twin flame is not looking for someone to take care of. A twin flame is looking for your wholeness to complement his own or her own, so that, when you are together as one complete Alpha/Omega circle, you can minister to life in need, to others who have not yet discovered the law of their oneness.

So, while you are aware of the fact that you are incomplete in some sense of the word, you lack this or that, you have to tie into the superior matrix of your wholeness which does exist and is now at inner levels. It is the wholeness of your Christ Self, the wholeness of your I AM Presence, and your absolute and eternal, divine union with your twin flame.

You need to affirm it right here. You need to have a sense of peace about present wholeness, and you can, because it exists right now in God where you are. When you have that peace, then and only then do you have something to offer anyone, any part of life.

When you have the peace of wholeness, all you can do is attract from the four corners of the heavens more of that wholeness, more of the confirmation of what you know you are and what you are in reality.

So, while you have a sense of filling in the matrix, while you have a sense that sooner or later you're going to fill that hunger, presently you affirm: "I am filled. I am full of Light."

By that affirmation, by that Divine *Be*-Attitude, you will attract every person, every condition, and every circumstance in your life that is necessary for the fruition of cosmic purpose. That may or may not include your twin flame, but it no longer matters because *you are your twin flame.* "I and my Father are One. I and my Mother are

One. I and my Twin Flame are One. We are One here and now!" *And you are never alone.*

That statement eliminates time and space, all distance and maya. It gives you peace and harmony. Because you know you are whole, you pull down from your Causal Body of Light and your I AM Presence all of the virtues and factors and talents and supply and abundance and beauty and joy and wisdom you need to be who you really are.

When you are that one, people are magnetized to you because of their own sense of need. You have, in manifestation in your aura, what they need. So they come. They come to be fed. They come to hear. They come to be nourished. They come to you for advice professionally. They come because you have something they don't have.

What you have is that very simple key

that "I AM THAT I AM. Here and now I AM One; We are One. Alpha and Omega are One where I AM. No time or space can separate me from my twin flame, for we are one in the Heart of God."

That is who everyone is seeking in life— the person who is whole and knows he is whole and uses his very wholeness to transmute the wants and lacks in the physical plane, the last vestiges of karma, and all of the various human situations that get left over and still have to be dealt with in our lives.

So that is the key to your union with your twin flame. And I think that that affirmation of Being is the starting point of an eternity of happiness.

Just remember, the mere absence of the quality of joy, of happiness, may be depriving you, in the outer sense, of more than you can ever dream of. So, just at the moment when you slip into a little sadness, a little self-pity, a little indulgence in mood energy— at that moment, remember: you may have lost the spark of contact with your twin flame.

Your twin flame doesn't deserve to have to experience your moods, your self-pity, and your self-indulgence. If you can understand the twin flame as the God-counterpart of you, and you have a sense of reverence for God in your life, you may look at yourself and say, "Maybe I'm not worthy now, but one hour from now I'm going to be worthy. I'm going to remake myself so that I'm irresistible to God, the angels, the Masters. They're going to walk and talk with me. They're going to enjoy being in my house. And my twin flame is going to seek and find me."

So, decide who you are. Decide what

you've got to do. Ask God. Then go out and find the people who are a part of your team —your group karma—for world service.

Let's be up and doing. It's only in action that we find God—God in ourselves and in our twin flame.

I love you!

I and my Father are One.
I and my Mother are One.
I and my Twin Flame are One.
We are One here and now!

THE CHART OF YOUR
DIVINE SELF

*Y*ou have a unique spiritual destiny. One of the keys to fulfilling that destiny is understanding your divine nature and your relationship to God.

To help you understand this relationship, the Ascended Masters have designed the Chart of Your Divine Self, which they also refer to as the Tree of Life. The Chart is a portrait of you and the God within you, a diagram of yourself—past, present, and future.

THE I AM PRESENCE AND CAUSAL BODY

The Chart of Your Divine Self has three figures, corresponding to the Three Persons of the Trinity and the Divine Mother. The upper figure corresponds to the Father (who is one with the Mother) and represents your I AM Presence. The I AM Presence is the Presence of God individualized for each of us. It is your personalized I AM THAT I AM, the name of God revealed to Moses at Mount Sinai.

Your I AM Presence is surrounded by seven concentric spheres of rainbow light that make up your Causal Body. The spheres of your Causal Body are the storehouse of everything that is real and permanent about you. They contain the records of the virtuous acts you have performed to the glory of God and the blessing of man through your many incarnations on earth.

No two Causal Bodies are exactly alike because their shimmering spheres reflect the unique spiritual attainment of the soul. The particular attributes you have developed in your previous lives determine the gifts and talents you will be born with in your succeeding lives. These talents are sealed in your Causal Body and made available to you through your Higher Self.

THE HOLY CHRIST SELF

Your Higher Self, or Holy Christ Self, is depicted as the middle figure in the Chart of Your Divine Self. Your Holy Christ Self is your inner teacher, guardian, and dearest friend. He is also the voice of conscience that speaks within your heart and soul. He divides the way between good and evil within you, teaching you right from wrong.

Shown just above the head of the Holy Christ Self is the dove of the Holy Spirit descending in the benediction of the Father-Mother God.

The shaft of white light descending from the I AM Presence through the Holy Christ Self to the lower figure in the Chart is the crystal cord. In Ecclesiastes, it is referred to as the silver cord (Eccles. 12:6). Through this "umbilical cord" flows a cascading stream of God's light, life and consciousness. This stream of life empowers you to think, feel, reason, experience life, and grow spiritually.

YOUR DIVINE SPARK
AND FOUR LOWER BODIES

The energy of your crystal cord nourishes and sustains the flame of God that is ensconced in the secret chamber of your heart. This flame is called the threefold flame or divine spark. It is literally a spark of sacred fire from God's own heart.

The threefold flame has three "plumes." These plumes embody the three primary attributes of God and correspond to the Trinity. The white-fire core from which the threefold flame springs represents the Mother.

As you visualize the threefold flame within you, see the blue plume on your left.

It embodies God's power and corresponds to the Father. The yellow plume, in the center, embodies God's wisdom and corresponds to the Son. The pink plume, on your right, embodies God's love and corresponds to the Holy Spirit. By accessing the power, wisdom, and love anchored in your threefold flame, you can fulfill your reason for being.

The lower figure in the Chart represents your soul. Your soul is sheathed in four different "bodies," called the four lower bodies: (1) the etheric body, (2) the mental body, (3) the desire body and (4) the physical body. These are the vehicles your soul uses in her journey on earth.

Your etheric body, also called the memory body, houses the blueprint of your identity. It also contains the memory of all that has ever transpired in your soul and all impulses you have ever sent out through your soul since you were created. Your mental body is the vessel of your cognitive faculties. When it is purified it can become the vessel of the Mind of God.

The desire body, also called the emotional body, houses your higher and lower desires and records your emotions. Your physical body is the miracle of flesh and blood that enables your soul to progress in the material universe.

The lower figure in the chart corresponds to the Holy Spirit, for your soul and four lower bodies are intended to be the temple of the Holy Spirit. The lower figure is enveloped in the violet flame—the transmutative, spiritual fire of the Holy Spirit. You can invoke the violet flame daily to purify your four lower bodies and consume negative thoughts, negative feelings and negative karma.

Surrounding the violet flame is the tube of light, which descends from your I AM Presence in answer to your call. (See p. 152.)

It is a cylinder of white light that sustains a forcefield of protection around you twenty-four hours a day as long as you maintain your harmony.

The Divine Mother focuses her energy within us through the sacred fire of God that rises as a fountain of light through our chakras. *Chakras* is a Sanskrit term for the spiritual centers in the etheric body. Each chakra regulates the flow of energy to a different part of the body. The seven major chakras are positioned along the spinal column from the base of the spine to the crown.

THE DESTINY OF THE SOUL

The soul is the living potential of God. The purpose of the soul's evolution on earth is to perfect herself under the tutelage of her Holy Christ Self and to return to God through union with her I AM Presence in the ritual of the ascension. The soul may go through numerous incarnations before she is perfected and is thereby worthy to reunite with God.

What happens to the soul between incarnations? When the soul concludes a lifetime on earth, the I AM Presence withdraws the silver cord. The threefold flame returns to the heart of the Holy Christ Self, and the soul gravitates to the highest level of consciousness to which she has attained in all of her incarnations.

If the soul merits it, between embodiments she is schooled in the retreats, or spiritual homes, of the Ascended Masters in the heaven-world. There she studies with angels and masters of wisdom who have gained mastery in their fields of specialization.

The ascension is the culmination of lifetimes of the soul's service to life. In order for the soul to attain this ultimate union with God she must become one with her Holy

Christ Self, she must balance (pay the debt for) at least 51 percent of her karma, and she must fulfill her mission on earth according to her divine plan. When your soul ascends back to God you will become an Ascended Master, free from the round of karma and re-birth, and you will receive the crown of ever-lasting life.

Note: You can place the Chart of Your Divine Self on your personal altar where you give your prayers and meditations as a focus of your divine reality (see page 158).

PRAYERS AND DECREES
FOR TWIN FLAMES

TO ARCHANGEL MICHAEL
FOR PROTECTION

Prayer

In the name of my Mighty I AM Presence, I call now for the victory of my twin flame, for the cutting free of my twin flame by the power of the mighty blue flame and sword of Archangel Michael. Legions of Light, come into action now!

Wherever my twin flame is, cut him/her free. Cut me free. Cut us free now to fulfill the divine plan and attain union in the level of the Christ, in the level of our chakras. And if it be the will of God, draw us together in a lifetime service. We thank you and accept it done this hour in full power according to God's will. Amen.

[Give this decree aloud three times or more with intense devotion, repeating the refrain after each verse:]

1. Light's protection manifest—
   Holy Brotherhood in white,
   Light of God that never fails,
   Keep us in thy perfect sight!

Refrain: I AM, I AM, I AM
              protection's mighty power,
          I AM, I AM, I AM
              guarded every hour,
          I AM, I AM, I AM
              perfection's mighty shower
          Manifest, manifest, manifest!

2. Lord Michael, mighty and true,
   Guard us with thy sword of blue.
   Keep us centered in the Light's
   Blazing armor shining bright!

3. Around us blaze thy sword of faith—
   Mighty power of holy grace,
   I AM invincible protection always
   Pouring from thy dazzling rays!

TO TRANSMUTE THE KARMA
OF TWIN FLAMES

Prayer

In the name of the Christ I call to the blessed I AM Presence of our twin flames for the sealing of our hearts as one for the victory of our mission to humanity.

I invoke the light of the Holy Spirit for the consuming of all negative karma limiting the full expression of our divine identity and the fulfillment of our divine plan.

[Recite the following violet-flame mantra and decrees three times each or in multiples of three. Visualize the violet flame surrounding you and your twin flame. See it cleansing your auras and instantaneously transmuting any negative energy into the light of God.]

I AM a being of violet fire!
I AM the purity God desires!

I AM THE VIOLET FLAME

I AM the violet flame
   In action in me now
I AM the violet flame
   To Light alone I bow
I AM the violet flame
   In mighty cosmic power
I AM the light of God
   Shining every hour
I AM the violet flame
   Blazing like a sun
I AM God's sacred power
   Freeing every one

RADIANT SPIRAL VIOLET FLAME

Radiant spiral violet flame,
  Descend, now blaze through me!
Radiant spiral violet flame,
  Set free, set free, set free!

Radiant violet flame, O come,
  Expand and blaze thy light through me!
Radiant violet flame, O come,
  Reveal God's power for all to see!
Radiant violet flame, O come,
  Awake the earth and set it free!

Radiance of the violet flame,
  Expand and blaze through me!
Radiance of the violet flame,
  Expand for all to see!

Radiance of the violet flame,
  Establish Mercy's outpost here!
Radiance of the violet flame,
  Come, transmute now all fear!

HEART, HEAD AND HAND
DECREES

Heart

Violet fire, thou Love divine,
Blaze within this heart of mine!
Thou art mercy forever true,
Keep me always in tune with you.

Head

I AM Light, thou Christ in me,
Set my mind forever free;
Violet fire, forever shine
Deep within this mind of mine.

God who gives my daily bread,
With violet fire fill my head
Till thy radiance heavenlike
Makes my mind a mind of light.

Hand

I AM the hand of God in action,
Gaining victory every day;
My pure soul's great satisfaction
Is to walk the Middle Way.

Tube of Light

Beloved I AM Presence bright,
Round me seal your tube of light
From Ascended Master flame
Called forth now in God's own name.
Let it keep my temple free
From all discord sent to me.

I AM calling forth violet fire
To blaze and transmute all desire,
Keeping on in Freedom's name
Till I AM one with the violet flame.

Forgiveness

I AM forgiveness acting here,
Casting out all doubt and fear,
Setting men forever free
With wings of cosmic victory.

I AM calling in full power
For forgiveness every hour;
To all life in every place
I flood forth forgiving grace.

Supply

I AM free from fear and doubt,
Casting want and misery out,
Knowing now all good supply
Ever comes from realms on high.

I AM the hand of God's own fortune
Flooding forth the treasures of light,
Now receiving full abundance
To supply each need of life.

Perfection

I AM life of God-direction
Blaze thy light of truth in me.
Focus here all God's perfection,
From all discord set me free.

Make and keep me anchored ever
In the justice of thy plan—
I AM the presence of perfection
Living the life of God in man!

Transfiguration

I AM changing all my garments,
Old ones for the bright new day;
With the sun of understanding
I AM shining all the way.

I AM light within, without;
I AM light is all about.
Fill me, free me, glorify me!
Seal me, heal me, purify me!
Until transfigured they describe me:
I AM shining like the Son,
I AM shining like the sun!

Resurrection

I AM the flame of resurrection
Blazing God's pure light through me.
Now I AM raising every atom,
From every shadow I AM free.

I AM the light of God's full presence,
I AM living ever free.
Now the flame of life eternal
Rises up to victory.

Ascension

I AM ascension light,
Victory flowing free,
All of good won at last
For all eternity.

I AM light all weights are gone.
Into the air I raise;
To all I pour with full God-power
My wondrous song of praise.

All hail! I AM the living Christ,
The ever-loving One.
Ascended now with full God-power,
I AM a blazing sun!

TEACHINGS, DECREES AND MUSIC
FOR YOUR MEDITATION ON
SOUL MATES AND TWIN FLAMES

TEACHINGS ON RELATIONSHIPS

**MARRIAGE AS AN INITIATION
ON THE PATH**
by Elizabeth Clare Prophet
2 audiotapes 1 hr. 33 min. #A95113 $14.95

TWIN FLAMES AND SOUL MATES
A New Look at Love, Karma and Relationships
by Elizabeth Clare Prophet
1 audiotape 90 min. #S86005 $8.95

HOW TO GIVE AND RECEIVE MORE LOVE
by Elizabeth Clare Prophet
1 audiotape 90 min. #B97075 $7.95

MUSIC CASSETTES

THE CROWNING ROSE
Songs of Love for All Seasons
1 audiotape 45 min. #B8213 $8.95

DECREE CASSETTES & CDs

LOVE MEDITATIONS
1 audiotape 70 min. #A95046 $7.95

HEALING MEDITATIONS
1 audiotape 70 min. #A94118 $7.95

SAVE THE WORLD WITH VIOLET FLAME I
1 audiotape 90 min. #B88019 $7.95

DEVOTIONS, DECREES AND SPIRITED SONGS TO ARCHANGEL MICHAEL
1 audiotape 70 min. #A93090 $8.95

WALLET CARD FOCUSES

TWIN FLAMES 2¼" × 3½" #4450 $1.00

THREEFOLD FLAME 2¼" × 3½" #2943 $1.00

VIOLET FIRE 2¼" × 3½" #2944 $1.00

CHART OF YOUR DIVINE SELF
2¼" × 3½" #1060 $1.00

CHAKRAS (set of 9): Heart Chakra, Secret Chamber of the Heart, Chakras in the Body of Man, Crown Chakra, Third Eye, Throat Chakra, Solar Plexus, Seat-of-the-Soul, Base-of-the-Spine
2¼" × 3½" #5007 $7.95

POSTERS

CHART OF YOUR DIVINE SELF
6" × 9"   #198 $1.50
15" × 26" #1404 $6.95

BOOKS

ACCESS THE POWER OF YOUR HIGHER SELF
Softbound 4"×6" 106 pages #4423 $4.95

**VIOLET FLAME TO HEAL BODY,
MIND AND SOUL**
Softbound 4"×6" 106 pages #4424 $4.95

NURTURING YOUR BABY'S SOUL
A Spiritual Guide for Expectant Parents
Softbound 233 pages #4448 $12.95

To request our free catalog or place an order
or for information about seminars and
conferences with Elizabeth Clare Prophet, write
Summit University Press, Dept. 2001, PO Box 5000,
Corwin Springs, MT 59030-5000 USA
or call 1-888-700-8087.
Fax 1-800-221-8307
(406-848-9555 outside the U.S.A.)
E-mail us at tslinfo@tsl.org
Visit our web site at www.tsl.org

Elizabeth Clare Prophet is a pioneer of modern spirituality. She has written such classics of spiritual literature as *The Lost Years of Jesus, The Lost Teachings of Jesus, Saint Germain On Alchemy, Reincarnation:*  *The Missing Link in Christianity, Kabbalah: Key to Your Inner Power* and *Quietly Comes the Buddha: Awakening Your Inner Buddha-Nature.*

Since the 1960s, Elizabeth Clare Prophet has been conducting conferences and workshops throughout the United States and the world on spiritual topics, including angels, the aura, soul mates, prophecy, spiritual psychology, reincarnation, the mystical paths of the world's religions and practical spirituality.

She has been featured on NBC's *Ancient Prophecies* and A&E's *The Unexplained* and has talked about her work on *Donahue, Larry King Live, Nightline, Sonya Live* and *CNN & Company.* She lives in Corwin Springs, Montana.